Dreaming

In Verse

the lyrical art of

Ted Kittell

GlobalEdAdvance
Press

DREAMING IN VERSE

the lyrical art of Ted Kittell

Copyright © 2013 by Ted Kittell

Library of Congress Control Number: 2013934378

DREAMING IN VERSE

the lyrical art of Ted Kittell

ISBN 978-1-935434-17-7

Ted Kitell 1934 -

Subject Codes and Description: 1. Poetry: American General POE 005010; 2. Poetry: Inspirational & Religious POE 003000; 3. Poetry: American - Native American POE 015000

Cover Design by Barton Green

Printed in Australia, Brazil, France, Germany, Italy, Spain, UK, and USA.

Published by

GlobalEdAdvance Press

www.gea-books.com

Dedication

This book is dedicated to my "Pop",

Arthur Callen Kittell, Sr.

He loved writing poetry.

§

Table of Contents

Spirit

The Dreaming

I close my eyes.
A mist forms in my mind.
I am falling into the land of Morpheus.
The dream begins.

I sense a gathering of all unconscious thought,
every unwritten line.
A raven comes to talk to me.
As the elf leads the way down a corridor.
He is taking me to see the Master.
The dream moves on.

The Master sits on his throne,
Long robes and white skin.
This is his world, the land of thought,
Hidden by sleep.
The dreaming begins to end as I
awake.

Spirit

Spirit is the power within me.
Spirit moves past my personality.
Spirit is my strength.
Spirit is all around me.

Normal ordinary things are sacred.
Fatherhood is sacred.
Motherhood is sacred.
Elders are sacred.

I see the spirit within.
Then in time I see spirit without.
I see spirit all around me.
In every thing I see there is spirit.

I need no eyes to see beauty.
I need no ears to hear beauty
The place of dreams is beauty
Love and strength are beauty.

It is well with my soul.
My inner soul is at peace.

The Spirit That Dwells Within Me

I share my spirit
I remember my spirit

My spirit connects with other people.
I am born with a sacred contract.

I have purpose to my life.
I am not a lost soul.

I found my spirit through adversity.
I have surrendered to my spirit.

I have gone from darkness to light.
I allow God's love to flow through me.

I strengthen the spirit that dwells in me.

Do Not Follow

Do not follow
Where the path may lead.
Go, instead, where
There is no path
And leave a trail

Hmmm…….

It alludes some completely.

It lights on others as gingerly as a butterfly.

It makes others dance upon a fine line.

Sanity is a funny thing.

My Angel

When I find there is no one to turn to
        And I am feeling - rather low.
When I have no one to speak to
        And I have no place to go.
 I go deep within myself
        To find that love that I know is there.
 I know then my Angel is here.
        I hear a voice telling me
        it will be fine.
Then the warmth
        Of the sun shines for me.
An Angel's love is
        always true.
All I have to do is call.
        My Angel will be with me.
My Angel will always
        see me through whenever I need
        my Angel.

Awareness

I am awareness
I am life
I am a point of knowing
With closed eyes, I still can see
Apart from my body
Apart from the sun and stars
The universe
It surrounds me
It passes through me
Light
A point of knowing
But still I am
Awareness
This world exists
It surrounds me
I will pass through it
And become awareness
Light
A point of knowing
I am awareness

A Thought

I am not positive
        That all my thoughts
            Are original.

I am positive that
        My thoughts are not
            Always wonderful.

Heck, I am just
        Glad that I can
            Think at all.

Gratitude

I Thank The Lord

Thank the Lord for loving me.
        When others do not.
I thank you Lord for staying with me.
        Until I part this world to be with you.
I thank you Lord for answering me.
        When I call upon you.
I thank you Lord for giving me
        Gifts all my life, both large and small.

Thank you Lord for keeping me
        Safe from harm.

Thank you Lord for holding me
        Gently in your arms,

When you cannot keep me from harm.

(Thanksgiving as I was growing up was the holiday when the family would all gather. We usually had over 40 people for the meal.)

Thanksgiving

Oh God when we have food,
> Help us to remember the hungry.

When we have work, help us to
> Remember those who do not.

When we have warm homes, help us to
> Remember the homeless.

When we do not have pain, help us
> Remember those who suffer.

And remembering, help us
> To overcome our complacency,
> And bestir my compassion,

Make us concerned enough
> To help, by word and deed,
> Those who cry out for what
> We take for granted.

God's Gift Of Love

Tis the season to be hopeful.

To give praises ever more.

To lift your voice in celebration

Be joyful of God's gift of love.

Prayer

Quiet Time

I need some quiet time with God.
        To help me through each day.
Time to read his word.
        Time to pray.
This quiet time will give me
        The strength I need
For all I must do this day.

Remember

I give all to God. I remember yet
        That God gave all to me.
Whatever I am, or have
        I owe all to him.

Joy And Peace

May you have joy and peace.

Your friendship is a special blessing to me.

May you have much success.

May you have the joy of new beginnings.

May you have the freedom to be.

May you have the true source of happiness.

May you have the love of life.

May you have respect for God manifest in your daily life.

Just A Little Prayer

Just a little prayer
Will ease my troubled mind.

This little prayer will touch God.
He will help me unwind.

The little prayer doesn't take much time.

When I am through I will be amazed
That things work out fine.

Nature

Bah Nah Mah (Navajo)

Ahg be ay meen ya
        bah nah mah
Ahg bi ay meen ya
        bah nah mah
Ahg be ay meen ya
        bah nah mah
Mee a mee ahg bi ay
        ee kule

(Translation)
Evidently

They ran away, one after another
        Evidently
They ran away, one after another
        Evidently
They ran away, one after another
        Evidently
There was a change
        Unbeknown to anyone

Navajo Signs

Navajo Indian
Making rings,
Rugs and bracelets,
Beautiful things,
Designs and markings,
Strange and queer,
Spotted with turquoise.
Like skies so clear;
Telling a story
Of olden days
Of Gods in glory
And all their ways;
Writing history
With designs
The way of a Navajo
Talking with signs.

Hunter

To yonder peak so sharp and clear, I slowly
wander, looking for deer.

In the valley below, curling smoke campfires
glow, looking for deer.

It is autumn time, leaves tumble down,
From oak, aspen, and cottonwood.

Leaves cover the ground.
Leaves are friends of the timid deer.

They stand and wait, with attentive ear.
They raise their heads and sniff the breeze.

My hunter's feet crumple fallen leaves.
Quick as a flash they scamper away.

My hunter's feet go down to the valley.
I will hunt the deer no more today.

The Fir Tree

A fir tree stands tall and alone
    On barren northern heights.

It slumbers in tall white cover
    Of freezing snow and ice.

Silently alone as if mourning.
    On hard rock the great fir.

Cottonwoods

Worn gray Cottonwoods

Cotton blowing in the wind.

Limbs reaching to the sky.

Asking God above

To send rain to the desert.

Tree Shadows

The shadows from a tree
      Make a pattern
It changes with the wind.
        Shadows in the moonlight
Are bright and clear.
       The shadows from a tree.

Melancholy

The New Beginning

I am feeling lost inside.
I await the arrival of what I don't know.

I am just patiently waiting.
Maybe it is happiness, sorrow, death.

With a twist of magic,
Deep inside me the happiness exists.

No one sees the real me.
All they see is sorrow.

The sorrow that wants to leave,
Be forgotten, replaced.

Replaced by no fear, happiness.
Maybe that is what I am waiting for.

The light at the end. The new beginning

My Anger

I have been robbed,
    robbed of everything.
My anger comes like
    a bolt of lightning.
Everything is confusion
    and not able to think.
Where is my understanding?
    What is reality?
Is reality as I perceive it?
    Is it not as it appears?
My anger has robbed me of myself.

Cow In Winter

Have you listened still on a desert hill
    At the close of a bitter day?

When the setting sun was in the clouds,
Was sent in an orange haze.

It is a cold white world with deep snow
    That covers the land.

Then the plaintive bawl of a cow
    Is the most lonesome sound of all.

Hope

I Believe

The sun is my freedom,
   The wind is my song,
The coming of morning
   When the nights are long.
When I see a rainbow
   After a storms end.
I believe with all my heart
   That miracles do happen.

Sing In My Soul

The human touch is most wanted.
            The touch of my hand in yours.

It means more to me than the
            things of this world.

These things will be gone.

The touch of your hand and
            The sound of your voice

Will always sing on in my soul.

Acceptance

Oh to know acceptance
        In a feeling sort of way.

To be known for what I am
        Not what I do or say.

It is good to be and loved
        For the person I am.

My heart cries out to be loved
        For the person who is really me.

Hope

I have hope, want to see it?

Don't look too hard, hope is very delicate.

Funny thing, Hope
If you have any or not.

You can feel it all over.
Pretend you have some too.

But be gentle, it is so very delicate.

We will be fine, but never lose hope.

One

One Moment of Beauty
      Can Change One Life

With One Look
      One Smile
      One Chance in a Lifetime

To Wonder If One Day
      One Wish
      For One Minute
      One Second
      One Touch
      One Hand
      In One Other

Will Last One Time
      Forever

Truth

Greatest Want

The greatest want of the world.
Is men and women who
            will not be bought or sold

Men and women who
            are true and honest.

Men and women who fear
and do not fear to call sin
            by its right name.

Men and women whose conscience is true
            to doing their duty.

Telling The Truth

It is better to be divided by the truth
    Than being united by lies.

It is better to speak the truth that hurts
    Than lies that brings false comfort.

It is better to be hated by telling the truth
    Than being loved for telling a lie.

It is better to be alone with the truth
    Than being wrong with the multitude.

I Never Walk Alone

I never walk alone.
At times I think I walk alone.

In my sorrow and despair
        Jesus always walks with me.

There is no hour that Jesus is not with me.

Jesus is by my side.
Though unseen Jesus is there.

Jesus is my friend and guide.
Whenever I think I walk alone.

I reach out and find the hand of Jesus
        to show me the way.

Jesus brings me peace of mind.

Faith In God

The Rewards Of Faith

Faith brings forgiveness.
        Faith brings salvation.

Faith brings peace.
        Faith makes us stronger.

Faith is a shield to protect.
        Faith will bring rewards.

Trust In God

Trust in God from day to day.
        Don't give in to despair.

Hold on to God's hand.

Let God lead the way.

Trust in God from day to day.

The Cross I Carry

I Carry a cross with me as a simple reminder
that I am a Christian.

This cross is not magic,
nor is it a good luck charm.

It will not protect me from harm.
This cross is not for the world to see.

It is a simple understanding between my
savior and me.

When I feel the cross it reminds me of the
price he paid for me.

This cross reminds me to be thankful for the
blessings I have every day.

This cross is a reminder of the peace I share
with all who know my master.

This cross reminds no one other than me that
Jesus is the Lord of my life.

Faith

Little words
>are measures of the faith we let grow.

Our daily satisfactions come
>with the degree of faith we show.

Believing is not what we are.

Believing is something that we do.

Faith is more than helping us
>when we are afraid.

Faith is also knowing in good times
>that God is near.

Faith is more than wishing and what we want;

Faith is also what we say and do.

I Will Not Remember

When the stars of heaven stand before me,
I will not remember the worries
  Of my past,
  The trials of my life,
  The time I shed tears,
  The troubles and the strife.
For I have before me the glories
  of the heavens spread above.
The meaning of it all
  will be softened by His love.

My Sunset

Time becomes more important
        As the years come and go.

God has brought me
        Through the deep valleys,
        Through the pain and strife.

God has been with me
        Through the times of joy.

God is nearer to me
        In the sunset of my years.

I go on
        Without fear
        Into my sunset.

Addendum

My book of poetry would not be complete without this addendum of thoughts of CAN NOT and CAN to help my readers understand their role in life.

§

CAN NOT

We have never done it before.

It is too complicated.

We do not have the resources.

It will never work.

There is not enough time.

We already tried it.

There is no way it will work.

It is a waste of time.

It is a waste of money.

We do not have the expertise.

Our members will not go for it.

It is good enough.

We do not have enough money.

We do not have enough room.

It is not going to be better.

It can not be done.

No one communicates.

Is it not time to go home?

I do not have any ideas.

Let someone else deal with it.

It is too radical a change.

It does not fit us.

It is not my job.

I can not.

CAN

We have the opportunity to be first.
Let us look at it from a different angle.
Necessity is the mother of invention.
We will give it a try.
We will reevaluate some priorities.
We learned from the experience.
We can make it work.
Think of the possibilities.
The investment will be worth it.
Let us network with those who have it.
Let us show them opportunities.
There is always room to do better.
Could be there is something we can cut.
Temporary space might be possible.
We must try it one more time.
It will be a challenge.
Let everyone give their ideas.
Tomorrow is the time to try.
I will come up with some ideas.
I am ready to learn something new.
Let us take a chance.
We should look at it.
I will be glad to do it.
I can.

About the Author

Ted Kittell has enjoyed writing poetry since his college days. His fascinating childhood growing up with the Navajos in New Mexico has influenced his poetry and added to his rich life experiences.

Dr. Kittell has five earned doctorates, three master's degrees, and a bachelor degree. He also has certificates from Harvard Graduate School of Business OPM and AACC Counselor. He was honored as a Scholar in the Oxford Society of Scholars.

Theodore H. Kittell has been admitted to the Bar to practice law in Minnesota and California. He is an expert witness in healthcare management, has been a consultant for the Tennessee Board of Health for Nursing Homes, and was a licensed Nursing Home Administrator. He has served on various health related boards and commissions, and is affiliated with many professional associations. Throughout his business career Ted was active in Kiwanis or Rotary Clubs and was recognized as a Paul Harris Rotary Fellow.

Dr. Kittell's work experience includes 27 years as a hospital executive, two decades of experience as a lawyer, and ten years experience as a consultant in healthcare, education and management.

www.ingramcontent.com/pod-product-compliance
Lightning Source LLC
Chambersburg PA
CBHW031528040426
42445CB00009B/452